D0540249

JANE DURAN

Breathe Now, Breathe

for Peter

All my very best wishes,
thank you for making my
visit to Totleigh Barton
so enjoyable.
Peace and inspiration!
Jane, 17 March 1999

ENITHARMON PRESS LONDON
1995

First published in 1995
by the Enitharmon Press
36 St George's Avenue
London N7 0HD

Distributed in Europe
by Password (Books) Ltd.
23 New Mount Street
Manchester, M4 4DE

Distributed in the USA and Canada
by Dufour Editions Inc.
PO Box 7, Chester Springs
PA 19425, USA

ISBN 1 870612 52 3

Second impression 1996

The text of *Breathe Now, Breathe* is set
in 10pt Walbaum by Bryan Williamson, Frome,
and printed by
The Cromwell Press, Broughton Gifford, Wiltshire

for Redha

Acknowledgements

Acknowledgements are due to the editors of the following
publications in which some of these poems, or versions of
these poems, first appeared: *New Statesman and Society,
The North, The Observer, Poetry Durham, Poetry London
Newsletter, Poetry Review, The Rialto, Spokes, The Times
Literary Supplement; As Girls Could Boast* (The Oscars Press,
1994); *Camden Voices* (Katabasis, 1990); *Greek Gifts*
(Smith/Doorstop Books, 1992); *New Writing 4* (Vintage in
association with the British Council, 1995); *Out of the Blue*
(Blue Nose Press, 1994); *Poetry Introduction 8* (Faber and
Faber, 1993); *What Poets Eat* (Foolscap, 1994); and *Boogie
Woogie*, a pamphlet of poems published by Hearing Eye, 1991.

The Enitharmon Press gratefully acknowledges a grant
from the London Arts Board towards the production costs
of this volume.

Contents

The Mere Pleasure of Flying

This has happened before:
the unlikely loading of my carcass towards sky,
a redistribution of weight
pulling up just under my arms – lifting me
over low munching things,
a scarf through a ring.

The ship leaves its harbour on spidery feet
past pine trees etcetera at the end of the promontory
and unlikely, unlikely – alone in the air
I strengthen against the blue tonnage, the stopping

and sweep past the tree where all fruits jangle.
The grape the banana the mango the apple
detach from their stems and hang independently.

From end to end of me, over house masses – flotillas –
octagonal cinemas, glass dreadlocks of winter,
the sky feathery, layered, tumbles alongside me
not remote now. I fly

past the silent in twos, the speakers in threes
in the parks and the alleyways, on the docks and the gangways,
with two jets of water from dragon-fish nostrils –
an end of day celebration for things grounded and cornered,
all looking up, amazed and unworthy

to see me struggling in my element,
panting, held fast against the sky.

Braided Rug

The all America rag rug
I hide my feet in
twists as the Hudson
has learned to twist
outdoing its clouds
of dust. It opens out –
as the Missouri offers
in flood and mire
its alms,
or the Potomac pulls
at its raggedy banks.

It braids blue-grey
with river-black, silver
for the rare winter stillness
as if left out all night
by the mountains.
The repeated stopped waters
creak with my weight.

The floorboards of our kitchen
are polished to a nicety.
I am nimble on these knots.
I speak all the riverland tongues
of my mother tongue.
My accent fathers me.
My voice is too loud –
even the heron, the herring gull
disappear.

In the middle of London
I am elsewhere. To the long gone,
to the dead in me
I cry breathe now, breathe.
I know my bailiwick.
I stand on my rug.

Camels

for Syra

On your first day of secondary school
we set off in a minicab.
I know you've been awake since dawn,
preparing, worrying in your room
blue and draped as a tent.
Your braids are tightly knit.
Hands in your lap.
The small red and white checks
of your collar stick out
over your grey wool coat
like the slightest mention
of candlelight in a village
before morning, that first voice.

The driver is Moroccan, lifts out
Andalus from the loudspeaker
to remind us of the shimmering world
beyond the school, its breathlessness
and turquoise particles never ceasing,
the camels with their wide-of-the-mark
and fluid sidestepping, blinking
with their great neutral eyelids
sand-light, night,
their own lives whirling within them
far from our own, on the way
to school in a minicab.

The school is still far,
floating over Regent's Park.
You take out your new pencil case
with nothing missing.
We trail the Andalus song
like a slow scarf, like a beach-tide
across the windows of the car.
We can see over the gates of the school.

11

The other children arrive –
they are all courageous.
You take the measure of them
when their camels drop to their knees
and they slide down the rugs,
the four corners slipping.

The older girls wait
at the top of the steps,
bend down tenderly,
ask your name.

The Slow Dance

The school lights up at night.
Miss Laurie stands by the gymnasium
door, greets us, her grey waves
snuggle against her head,
frail as water, or a nightingale's
cry. A slow dance begins.
'No cheek to cheek!' she says,
taps our shoulders.
Our ears unhook.

We raise our eyes to heaven
but we know her.
In class she is severe
moving between our desks,
curious about the way we learn,
how each of us bends far down
into the equations, splits
them open so they breathe
like fresh timber in a forest
of living things.
She never belittles us.
Her voice is an algebra whisper.

We step back, half a foot
between us, till my red wool dress
and your blue suit bereaved of me
draw out the fine force,
manage the distance.

The door opens and snow comes in
with the boys, and she sees herself
again, years ago,
when she leaned against a mantelpiece
and a young man in an armchair
stood up to go and her waist,
the miracle of her waist,
was gathered in by sashes.

Navigator

Already he's American.
He lies down in his cabin.
His head touches one end
his feet the other.
A starfish with all its arms out
feels and feels a rock.
This is what patience is.

He followed the charts first
and now they follow him.
Already he's famous,
a headdress set with gold
teetering with the far-up
feathers of the universe.

He thinks of the tiny bowed
mainland windows,
light yellow as timber.
His clothes are twisted.
The wind will kill him.
Already he has a city
at the end of a river
mild as a calf.

He wakes up in the night
and touches his burning forehead.
Already his room drags at land,
the ledges of seaweed where nobody matters.

When I Slept

It rained all night. The rain drew me a picture.
He came to see me. He was incomparably young.
My mother was old now, sitting in her chair
in Cambridge. She did not know he was back.
He picked me up. His suit was wool,
he held me against that suit. The sea was 1950.
He was bright as an earring against my ear.
He spoke in long lines, I in short.

He had never been dead, here all along
just away and we forgot, the sole sailor
of the rain. His face was large, mine was tiny.
The slipped relic in the museum, under glass,
doggone, field gate wide open. Who would want
to sing anymore at the piano or tour
our living room, so many days without him?
He drags his boat along the mud flats,
he toils in the bay light and does not complain.
His daughters are tender, his daughters
love him tenderly, young man of the wigwam.

He clears his glasses from the side table,
his book of Don Quixote is open at that page
where he laughed on the last night of his life.
Back to be absent again, like a cold cry,
the cold piano keys seeping away, the rain drying,
the oxen stepping out from the drying
mud oh just outside my window.

Returning

I fly close to home with you,
summering, wintering
over the shingled houses.
Along the coast
a storm has picked at the berries
and the flags on the sailboats
are always beginning
their long wandering out.

When you slide your hand down my arm
like that, in the night,
what is dangerous and gentle
joins – two sides of a roof
that the sky slides down
pitching roses.

On the roof my heart spins timorously
like a weathervane.

To a Woodlouse

Magellan had nothing on your
ferocious legs channelling a carpet

as if tugging at a zodiac
just overhead, in the moist air.

I take your meaning –
our house has damp

behind the skirting-boards
harbouring you.

Such continents you pass
in the living room, sensing

where the wet loosens things.
Asia's leaf-litter is plummeting,

its temples unnerved, powdery.
The Americas are soft, disintegrating

those noble barns jittery.
The watermark of Europe is rising –

its splinter-rot, the black pines
you discover, leave behind.

You roll up your innermost
being like bedding, like a sunset

that can never know desert,
the dry damning wind. At night,

when the kitchen floor deepens
so there is no end to it,

your sailing skirts set out,
your fairy motor gnashing the tides.

17

The Man

There is a man in the house
behind ours – he roars.
His roar comes across the gardens.
His anger is inviolable.
There is a medieval moat
round that man in the house.
The apostolic hairs on his chest
are many.

When I wake up I hear him
down the years, the sole
witness of his pain.
His family have scattered,
his little girls
their chromosomes dancing round him
like ballerinas.
He will do nothing but roar
over a mistake, spilt milk.
His heart is in it.

If there were tambourines
triangles, drums, pianofortes
cymbals, that man in the house
would muster them,
yell his cobalt yell
among them. He needs to know
how to be most loud –
a mayor, town crier
a matted bell-ringer
suffering the cloud roofs.

He whirls his frayed edges
from room to room
letting them know
there is a man
a man around the place.

10 pm

This is the moment when
I go to the top of the house,
remove the iridescent bubbles
from my hands, stop everything.
I climb to the Russian blue evening
the opportunity of the cupola
the thirsty hour
where I can drink large clear thoughts.
I start the long walk up.
Perhaps I will not arrive.
Perhaps the roof will not imagine me.
Perhaps you will forget
to visit me there.

Zebra Zebra

A zebra lies out on the flatlands
in extremis, tinctured.
It has swum in a storm.
All its head is pulled back as if listening.
The ink steals into its ears.

Three lion cubs find the zebra.
Their shirt-tails are out.
They have come through the long grass
tussling, tumbling
past the heartbeat of their mother.

The sun dumps its white-blue over the path.
The cubs walk over the zebra's india ink,
their good fortune, jump its legs,
hesitate on the brink. The zebra's
breath has gone back to the plain, the pollen.

They do not yet know
how to tear and devour,
but the zebra is surprising
as a child sees henna at a wedding
on a hand, a foot,

or the river leaves behind
its fiery pattern in the silt,
the story of how it bore away
the naked fish. I lifted my book of poems
from the deep box one Christmas.

I was lame with a piece of glass in my foot.
I took the *Songs of Innocence
and of Experience* into the kitchen,
away from the other children.
How slyly the words were chosen

you could whisper them –
those dazzling lines drawn painstakingly
across a life, like losses.

Travelling Boat from
the Tomb of Meket-Re

The funeral boat
makes light
in its glass case,
sweeps downriver,
its little oars
brandishing,
in the Egyptian section
of the Metropolitan Museum,

stirs the fringes
of a palm tree,
collides freely
with a procession of reeds,
enters the cloudmost
bend of river
at this appointed time.

Intrepid
the river people
glitter in their boat,
with no commotion
or word against the rotund
thumbprint of dark
stunning the entrance
to the tomb.

This travelling boat
from the tomb of Meket-Re
is studied by children
who twirl on their handsome
roller-skates in Central Park
and who have already received
many answers to many questions
in their short lives.

Stonewalling

The donkey stares
into a hole
blown through the sky
by the sun at noon.

He has been loaded
with rocks, hauled
by the reins, struck
with a stick

and has set off
at a pace.
But now, halfway
down the mountain

the donkey lurches
and stops,
gathers his power
to be still

among the fragrances
of thyme and oregano
lifting like a cathedral,
the sound of spaces

milling in his ears.
He could wait
in the same spot
till the stars kick up

and the furnished slopes
disappear on a mere
breath and the men
take up his burden,

humbled with walls.
The eyes that turn,
hardly noticing the deeps,
are like the little streets

you enter suddenly,
had not supposed were there,
from the chief square.

One Summer

My fat landlord with his white shoes
sits at his table in the café...
He has chosen the noisiest avenue.
We have to shout to be heard.
I say 'What?' and he describes his youth,
a girl he loved at that time, from his area.
'She was shy', he says. 'Her sister...'

My landlord has stopped speaking.
A young couple walk past the café, entwined,
slowly under the trees, through the crowd.
The girl has long black hair, a raspberry blouse.
The awning makes red and yellow stripes
across our table. A pitcher of water shimmers.
'What was I saying?' he asks, calling for the waiter.

Courtesan

A blue silk chair,
yellow square through the slats,
slander of light.

A sturdy bottle of perfume
tied with a red tassel.
Fist, fist of pearls.

She dwells on her possessions
at moments in the conversation
over lunch, and drawing

a fishbone from her teeth
recalls how the rainborn
snap of sun

demeaned her skin
in the mirror this morning.
A grave walking-stick

leans against the wall
in the dark turning-point
of the hall.

It is already the late
afternoon of a lion
opening its jaws,

high fire of a cathedral.
Winter has never entered this room.
The decline is gradual.

The White Toothbrush

for Thomas Fanourakis

The white toothbrush
is laid neatly
along the top ledge
of the wooden mirror-frame.

I have been sleeping in your room
while you are in hospital.
Your bed is no wider than me.

Here your paintings of women
softly look out beyond me,
warm, with their own concerns
in their faces

and your paintbrushes
in the metal pitcher
with all the paint and turpentine
washed out, washed right out
so they are clean and pure perhaps

as the air outside the closed café
long before dawn,
as if they had never painted anything.
They have been like that for years.

Those women in grey and dark green
gaze out into their existences
as if they could reach out into the traffic
of Heraklion starting before morning:
the shutters bound for heat

the way the buses are bound for the villages
and go deep into the mountains
to remind them of the practical
duties of their lives,
that first task – a plate, a cup.

By my bed is the pale lemon jug, worn
with the clay pressing through the simple design
of brown brushstrokes, through to the end.

Time Zones

It will be cold now in Crete.
They will be pulling out
from the chests the locked-in
rugs. They will draw in
from the trees for needy
breakfasts. The sheep will blur.

It will be dark and never
dark in New York, this time.
Streets will speed by
with their ice lights
hurting. Bar doors
will be half open,
the rich light dropping its force
on the sidewalk
like the girl in a blue
leotard, collapsing to rest
on the dance studio floor.

In Bangladesh it will be afternoon
already. All the afternoons
that have ever been
will be in it, of it.
The entrances to villages
will be jugs
turned inside out –
smooth lemon walls,
pathways – the rub of ginger.

In Peru couples will be asleep
in the presence of mountains,
of heavy rivers.
Hardly a match will burn
in the Andes, the extinguishing
torrents.

Torrents will happen,
wind, ice.
In all these places we have been
there will be no trace of us.

River

The boat carries merchandise
slowly downstream,
past signalling long grass.
A town is waiting
far away, drying its roofs
by the edge of the water,
calling in its fish.
The boat searches for the pale
blue and brown verticals of wood,
the families gentle on doorsteps,
and the town is attentive to the river
murmuring the motor in its mud.

The Wonderful Belly Dance of Rabah Saïd

When Rabah dances
in his tiny apartment
on the outskirts of Malmö
his friends round the coffee-table
witness
his belly imperious.

When he shimmies
between the television set
and the picture window

landmarks surface out of the fog.
At the black docks
the lights of the ferry to Copenhagen
turn on all at once.

He unbuttons his shirt.
He locks his hands behind his head
whirls and shudders on the spot

and the last stars leap
between branches of fir trees.
Over the fleeting farmlands
barn doors open
to let out their dark.

In sedate parade meanders
the gleam of cattle haunches
and breath has an edge of snow
an edge of sirocco

like two cusps of the moon
when Rabah lifts up his arms
and laughs down at his dancing belly
over the astonished
rooftops of Malmö

and a young bridegroom, lying awake
remembers a riddle
from his childhood
when Rabah spins down the hallway

gliding, eddying
across the marine snow of Sweden:
a sandstorm at dawn,
his red shirt – banners.

The Horses in the Gaucho's Head

The horses I know well
are the glazed Chinese horses
of Manhattan hallways
with their grief manifest –
hocks and the manes
with their tiny weights.
Or the splayed legs
of Peruvian clay horses,
lame with the mud they come from.
The chalk and ebony horses of Chile
who have named the districts
they passed through, fair
and reeking of sun and silence.
The rider with his legs clasped round.

But the horses in the gaucho's head
are invisible presences
or pale blue profiles
you can put the palm of your hand over
like memories of manes.
He knows how to run with them –
those wary horses he wants to tame
king-kicking the yellow dust,
the startled grass of the plain
or galloping together like a tenderness
that overcomes the senses all at once,
a riverboat bearing down on the morning.

Then when the gaucho is resting
he stands in the deep shade,
a stone or two by his toe,
as if to say 'Leave me in peace'.
As if he could sleep on his feet too,
or gaze out with the coal eyes of God
from the trees.

Stillborn

This hurt has beat so long,
turns up with the tide
each month – memorial.

The midwife waits by the bed.
A hand rests on my belly,
trails its design
with sympathy.
Who weeps with me?
I do not recognise
the long white hair.

Bygone – the fire escape,
a point of entry,
a wedge.
The fire hand is austere
all night long
all labour long
undoing.

I touch your foot
before you go
stepping blindly off
no toehold, no notches
to catch at
nothing binding, nothing soft

our child
dropped down through time
through the slats
like a dime.

Here in my bed
I exchange coinage with the night.
The curtain whisks up – seagull edge,
its white barely flaring.
The roof is smitten with rain
and the ends of stories.

Miscarriage

The womb refused,
backed up,
its particles of silk
wasted, perish.
Breathless –
the cloudy silo,
the yolk sea.

In the ceremony
of lifting
and enclosing
the womb refused.
The ceremony of no-child
followed.

On either side
its ostrich neck
its camel neck
wavered,
swallowed the high
midnight.

The womb held back.
It had an eye
for sand,
spread its cool
oranges and reds
on dry land,

and bright
and fierce
as a lair,
the womb bear-hugged
its dead,
and let go.

Termination for Fetal Abnormality

Icing or sand?
This shoreline is sweet.
I snuggle into pregnancy
careful, canny
to keep the bubble floating,
soft loop under my belly button.
Thumb and index finger in an O
where the veins show through.
Summer's an eel
pitching, a landing seal.
I'm bleary-eyed.
The purposes of the heart
smart and slide.

But now the cautious voices
have come alongside me
with the news.
The reeds have been tied together
like teepees in the wild violet
storm sky.
The further out they take you
the more I try to follow:
you come close, stop short,
turn away before I can feel
your breath on my hand.
The lamps are held low over me
as they search the river of my tongue
for your name, Ismail.

Forty Eight

Once a month I expect that I am pregnant.
My body takes that liberty –
in the street I am full of misgivings, armfuls,
my breasts manage the joy of being painful.

I expect that the gleaning has taken hold,
the warrior gates have closed
and the town turned heavy inside
with its gold, its tarnish of silver.
I expect the little known
to be drumming and corded,
my belly to be amazed and striated
with new boundaries.

There will be no going back,
once a month.
Nowhere will the bereft be local.
They will not be in their usual cafés.
They will be overlooking seaports
and their voices will drop with evening
so as not to wake the children.
No one will be childless
nor the haze hide a bay.

There are slip landings in my belly,
the tug of the mollusc love,
its impersonal kiss unfolded
its wish-kiss lying low
left behind when the sea goes out and stops
for my foot to go oops on the slippery rock.

When the blood lies out on its shoal,
when the blood arrives
on the sloop, on the stoop, like a sailor,
like an acrobat, like electricity,
I will say it is not really that.
No, no. I am not ready.

The Pumpkin at Halloween

My niece carried a pumpkin
down the supermarket aisle.
She rolled and bumped it
across the night for fun,
down the sticky rain streets
though it was very heavy,
churning and charming as it was
with seedlore and threads,
held it in her arms
staggering slightly
under a streetlamp
and put it down
outside some council flats
and sat on it. At home
she dug the pumpkin out,
peeked into its mathematics,
its seeds interminable,
its double dealing,
its wild lapping inner walls,
tugged at its sunk city,
jolted days and weeks out of it,
tipped the darkness
from its eyes and mouth.
In the middle of its sunset land
we lit a candle for the pumpkin,
its forgotten trails,
its medallion oceans,
pored over the long words
it released on the wall.
Once the pumpkin lay in a field,
edible and quilted,
chiming softly.
Now it burns in a child's autumn,
ferocious and hollow.

Three in the Morning

At three in the morning
when you come to bed
from the well of downstairs
where you have been working
for hours at your computer
as if underwater, its blurred
blues and greens, the computer
which mirrors the universe
with its floating numbers,
its dots of existence,
its embedded knowledge
and symbols branded lightly
brushed against the earth –
fossils, cave paintings,
scripts position themselves,
lift and fall, mortal
as the space circumscribed;
and I have just fallen asleep
after a few lines of a poem
have come to me,
the breath of a poem
I had not understood till now,
we turn to each other
with all the secrets of this world.

Boogie Woogie

Soap-edge shoes slip nine ways
in the gymnasium, awake all night.
We have opened the small windows at the top,
goblets of stars in a blur.

The girls, the fellows on the steps.
We discover the night porcupines
in the grass, the slopes of fireflies.
The geranium gymnasium calls us back.
We cannot sleep. We cannot sleep.

We line up along the walls
in blue chiffon, in tucks and frills,
with sad bony shoulders, in pale lemon shoes

we spin out along the polished floor
all the mosquito folly of the dance.

Small Town

The movie house opened early
after church. A few faces
lit up in the dark.
Each smiled the smile
of a mouth on another mouth,
trailed smoke across the entrance.
You can smell the rain coming
down the streets, rattling,
opening and closing screen doors.

Let it all appear
as it was then –
the shacks and wires
and car tires and shop signs
and clicking of heels in the street.
The girl sitting outside a shop
looking down the hill
over black roofs,
the girl with her back to me.

Why didn't I see
that this is all there is –
just a few miles off the highway?
I couldn't tumble it out.
I couldn't divide it
into pieces of language,
languid in my bare feet
in the dark five-and-ten-cents store.

All dawn the road into town
stretches across my dream –
an orange cloth
pulling in a young deer
to the very edge, to the first houses,
from the blue fir trees, out there.

New Hampshire Thunderstorm

In the attic I found inkwells
belonging to my grandmother,
anchors running warm with water, stars.
Weights for her paper, hemispheres.

The thunderstorm came across New Hampshire
across the porch, across the rugs.
Soldier storms deleted, deleted.

Small the forest basket,
small the threads of oak,
birch cries, tubs of rusty water.

When it rained up from the ground
purple clover flowers were driven
over the grass, spinning and stunned,
onto the apron of our house.

I sat on the porch with my grandmother
in the white wicker, watching the weather.
How far back from here
the thunderstorm which delighted us,

which slipped like a nosegay under our chins
and tore us away from each other.

Migrations

How eagerly the spiny
lobsters rush
through the blue water
till they are
transparent too.

They mark the worst tidings
and set off,
queue for deep water
tail-to-antenna
so the sea floor
seems and seems
ahead, opening out
and descending.

At the great ocean drop
rolling, dark and agreeable
borne out, borne in,
each continues down alone

till the storm is high and remote
overhead
and passes feelingly
in the reef.

That is the main thing –
getting away in time
where autumn tumbles
right through the bright reef
like letters sent
'Come home! Come home!'

Bare into cool, cooler, cold
slow, slower, everything clean
reaped, blacker

to the depth
where the heart can stand
stillness, safety,
rumour the way back
to a higher country.

For the Woman Who Dressed Up
to Listen to Gigli on the Radio

On her evening off
she put on her green silk
dress loose at the waist
with tiny pleats flaring
at the wrists
and below the knee.
She tidied the sitting-room
right above the kitchen
and turned on the radio
to listen to Beniamino Gigli.

Downstairs the family
made do without her,
took the ham from the fridge,
shook out the tablecloth,
left the dishes in the sink.
There was no need
to do them. Outside the snow
was falling, the voice of
Gigli beginning.

The lamp unburdened
its light into the room.
Her manuscript of silk shone.
She did not understand
the Italian when Gigli sang
to her and her alone,
ah! completely alone with him.

Mr Teller the Piano Teacher

He stood by the piano for an hour, every Wednesday
he took Amanda's plump fingers and pressed them on the keys.
Clumsy entrances: the notes dragged out their prey
from all corners of the house.

A mother opened the door to the kitchen to hear better.
She wore the same dress always, with blue roses
here and there. Tinkle, crash – the dishes and the piano.
A father hummed the tunes, lagging behind.

A sister with a wide belt too tight to breathe properly
and a stone digging into the nape of her neck, ran upstairs,
slammed the door of her bedroom. The arpeggios stumbled
round and round that house with closed windows.

After the lesson Mr Teller, knowing the secrets of the sonata,
sat down to play for a few moments, just a few,
to show Amanda what he could have been,
what she could be, one day.

Music of stairwells, music dripped from inkwells.
The notes were for him. Those Wednesday evenings
when he sat at the piano thinking of himself as he was
then, of his student room matted with night

and how he opened the casement
how the pointed roofs, the largeness of snow held him.

Obsessive-Compulsive Disorder

It comes on slowly
the doubting illness
checking, checking
checkerboard, stepping

first in the dark, then the light
off, on,
the gas, the water.

Outside the rooster is crowing
and leaves will fly back to the wrong
side of the railway track.
They do things like that.

As if the apple-tree
could fast when it rains,
the winter stop short,
indoors there are rituals
against loss, against change.
So much has been taken from you
the horse already bolted

but there is always more
to be taken – blown across the yard
like chicken-feed, seed, cloud,
an empty stable hidden
behind the windy
flowershow.

Stare at the oven,
the lights, the taps,
the cooker. Count to thirty.
Are there stirrings?
Off, off, off, off.

Turn away, turn back,
peer into the stable.
Those cracks of light
are pond, lake, afternoon,
the horse gone.
Read the hay-dark, doubting.

Expatriate*

Ferreting, tapping the source
on my verandah, alone all morning.
A light rain falls.
Across the tops of trees
the white pavilion has the shine of bone.

The ape of land has me in its arms.
I curl my breath round each month
exhaled by this land.
Why did you ask me to stay?

Here are poppy shades
and princely yellows.
I'm wound round with woollen skeins.
As I walk to and from the club
I am compact in my isolation.
See – the insect needles bounce off me.

I ring a bell and wish up a servant
and leather lychees on a tray.
He wants to join his uncle in Kuwait.
Along the mountain ledge
the train will stop
but lets no people off.

The First Wife

Hers was the smallest palace
open at all sides
facing his across a pool.
Chronicle of her life
passing across open and closed spaces
her eyes half-closed.
She had no sons.

Under a cool cloud
she visited the saint's tomb
carrying jasmine, tied orange
ribbon on the latticework with a wish,
drank the mildest teas,
made love with her head towards
the Pole Star, her feet in Orion,
and whispered the verses of a well-known
poet of the time to induce
the ecstatic state they say
is conducive to love
and the birth of sons.

A tongue writes a prayer
in the mouth, and there are rumours
across a listless courtyard.
At dusk the white animals
of the marble tomb
rise above a landscape
without form or colour.

After the first wife
how can there be another?
So why are the stonemasons building palaces
to please the foreign brides
arriving at night from other valleys,
from the lanterns of their fathers' houses,
in bruised silk, with downcast eyes?

Indian Miniature

This heat is so enormous
it drowns all her certainties.

It stalks her like a blue deer
into the forest, a grumpy cheetah.

It steps out in gold
from her palace room at night

on the verandah. It has a delicate
ring of bad temper.

It gives her an unwanted
hug. She calls her handmaidens.

Why has the princess
left her lover with such sudden

energy, to wait here
where what might be

might be only a disclosure
of breeze over her guava drink

or the excitement of sunrise
or dewfall,

looking over the wall
in her red tangled silk

down at the black night
full of stars and disguises

as if she were lowering a bucket
into a well?

Conversations with Lois

I like the fact that our most important conversations are held
    in the sea,
that I wear an electric blue swimsuit and you a yellow sarong
so we can identify each other between revelations and relatives.
Whole families pass between us up to their waists in foam, pink
boogie boards and neon. We discuss childlessness.
Our shoulders are hidden, our faces become memories for
    minutes.
You tell me about your new lover. A wave grows up behind us
and beautifies into a mist, universal and funny. Your listening –
and the whole sea is aware. *Illnesses, what he said to her,
regretted*... unintelligible. We use words like *forever*
and *searing*. Our stories pass into salt, crystallise.
We're distracted by goosebumps, seaweed, undertow, nylon
cradle-tents on the edge of collapse, cliffs. Aunts, cousins
wade in intelligently. How we know of no book readable
at this moment but this one, engaged in our meanings.
How there is nothing we say that is not water and air.

Snow Pudding

One way is to pour maple syrup
on fresh snow. Find a corner
by the house that the wind misses.
Do not dream of it but do it –
syrup that drifts from the maple,
your sticky mittens.

Or sprinkle gelatine over water,
add sugar, lemon. Heat gently.
It seems so effortless
like the minnows that will appear
in the pond this summer,
so many tourings against rock,

remedies, quickenings
or the powerful states of shade
under the waterfall.
Beat the egg whites – fold in
to bring the snow that races,
the doe at the window.

In grandmother's kitchen
there is an ooze from the oven dish
with the Atlantic in it,
a hush over it,
an invisible recipe
at the back of the cookbook –

how to prepare snow
when it is really taking you sideways
out of control –
past the side of the house
past the lost barn, journeying
with the blurred crossings

everywhere the land still rising.
Bring in your black and white branches.
Lay your icy clouds on the table.
The roads are impassable.

The Great Plain

It takes a fierce dog
to keep them to their imaginary
circle.

The sheep move forward
a blade of grass at a time –
their parked faces.
The snow mountains behind
applaud their births
and deaths.

Abandonment of place
makes their wool
grow deep.
Clouds shear the land.

It is so quiet
it could be Sunday.
The air rushes through their wool.
The ground is stone.
They have run out of field.

The shepherd makes a penitent
movement sideways.
The wind stops him here –
the great doors of this plain

you can throw yourself against
and call and call
and no one hears you.

The Orange Tree in Córdoba

The gradual branches
just made out, grains, smudges,
the orange tree, its energy
behind a wall where children
gather, its sticky, searing juices,
its dust coming from nowhere
like a moment of sadness,
its branches laid softly
against women, like menstruation.

A girl comes down the steps.
There are summers still in her,
there is oil and bead on her.
She holds her child's hand.
Lavenders wash the streets
with their browns in the early
mornings in Córdoba.

To the cry of the childless
the orange tree answers with fruit,
to the suppressed cry of the childless
the mementoes of its armfuls,
to the red and white striped arches
of the womb, the sky hurrying past
the lilies of the womb, it answers
'There is nothing more to be done.

The long robes of air
drag the earth like bloodstains
like the caked hoofs of horses,
the blacksmiths harrying the horseshoes,
the Moors leaving Córdoba endlessly.

Nine-month, nine-month lanterns
never so extinct as now.
Go into the Mosque.
Feel the power of space inside you,
the insatiable leaf-turning hand.'

Link

You look like early man.
I can feel the forest quaking
with the force of your foot,
the mica of your timidity,

the foot that anthropologists
have been shirring together
with their pencil brushes
on a hillside, noticing the pain

you might have felt pressed against
a stone, and how the skeletal
toes could bend and the arch
grip. For this is the furthest

cinnamon of earth, the poor
sand grains of gully, desert,
for you follow me everywhere.
The hands – near misses

on a hillside where the
lake crater shimmered.
All those anthropologists
from Ethiopia and America

brushed away the diamond
grains with their own right
hands in which the bones
judge together so perfectly

and lovingly the fine mess
of dry earth sifted, sifted.
This finding you.
In the intimacy of your desert

they stood up, and their knee joints
locked and gave so they could walk back
to the tent on two legs.
When the sun went down

over the tent they lit lanterns
and gulped coffee from a thermos.
They grasped the paper cups
easily and carried them across

the small space
and stood around in groups,
embracing with a fine joy
to see how you came

to this earth, and left again.

Great Grandfathers

for Henry Crompton

Sometimes you glimpse one –
a great grandfather –
among the trees
with his white hair blown forward
seated and secret,
glad to see you there
only just higher than his knees,
the checkered blanket,
sugar-line of the rivermouth
on his mouth.

You can hardly remember, later.
You were only four when he died
and neither of you in full faculties
when you met, so your greeting
was really a goodbye:
a blanket, leaves, a scrap of beard,
a river happening to a beach,
your heaven against his.

Still, when you think of him
he is tall, he is broad
as if he were set about with himself,
as if all the forests of Lancashire
had been used to build him.
He lones in his age.

His age is becoming fabulous.
Your mother says if he were alive now
he would be 102.
And there is that bundle of letters
he left behind
which you are only allowed to touch
with the delicacy of a ladybird alighting –
so brittle, so see-through.

Great, he is greater than your father,
grandfather, less great than his.
You think of going backward
like the sandpiper chasing the lost wave
wrestling with the tide
adept and forlorn
or how the balloon breath rushes back into
your mouth when you are trying
very hard to blow it up
to take to the park,
how it could blow you all the way back
right against his heart.